In summer, a grizzly bear trundles across the tundra of Denali National Park in Alaska. Previous page: In Utah's Canyonlands National Park, hellish summer heat is assuaged by the cool grace of Angel Arch.

LIFE
Our National Parks
Celebrating America's Natural Splendor

LIFE

Editor Robert Sullivan
Creative Director Ian Denning
Picture Editor Barbara Baker Burrows
Executive Editor Robert Andreas
Associate Picture Editors Christina Lieberman, Vivette Porges
Senior Reporters Hildegard Anderson, Anne Hollister
Copy JC Choi (Chief), Wendy Williams
Production Manager Michael Roseman
Picture Research Lauren Steel
Photo Assistant Joshua Colow
Consulting Picture Editors
Suzanne Hodgart (London), Tala Skari (Paris)

Publisher Andrew Blau
Director of Business Development Marta Bialek
Finance Director Camille Sanabria
Assistant Finance Manager Karen Tortora

Editorial Operations Richard K. Prue (Director),
Richard Shaffer (Manager), Brian Fellows, Raphael Joa,
Stanley E. Moyse (Supervisors), Keith Aurelio, Gregg Baker,
Charlotte Coco, Scott Dvorin, Kevin Hart, Rosalie Khan,
Po Fung Ng, Barry Pribula, David Spatz, Vaune Trachtman,
Sara Wasilausky, David Weiner

Time Inc. Home Entertainment

President Rob Gursha
Vice President, Branded Businesses David Arfine
Vice President, New Product Development Richard Fraiman
Executive Director, Marketing Services Carol Pittard
Director, Retail & Special Sales Tom Mifsud
Director of Finance Tricia Griffin
Assistant Marketing Director Ann Marie Doherty
Prepress Manager Emily Rabin
Book Production Manager Jonathan Polsky
Associate Product Manager Jennifer Dowell

Special thanks to Bozena Bannett, Robert Dente,
Gina Di Meglio, Anne-Michelle Gallero, Peter Harper,
Suzanne Janso, Robert Marasco, Natalie McCrea,
Mary Jane Rigoroso, Steven Sandonato

Published by

LIFE Books

Time Inc.
1271 Avenue of the Americas,
New York, NY 10020

ISBN: 1-931933-31-6
Library of Congress Control
Number: 2003100211

"LIFE" is a trademark of
Time Inc.

We welcome your comments
and suggestions about LIFE
Books. Please write to us at:
LIFE Books, Attention:
Book Editors, PO Box 11016,
Des Moines, IA 50336-1016

If you would like to order any
of our hardcover Collector's
Edition books, please call us
at 1-800-327-6388 (Monday
through Friday, 7:00 a.m.–
8:00 p.m. or Saturday, 7:00
a.m.–6:00 p.m. Central Time).

Please visit us, and sample
past editions of LIFE, at
www.LIFE.com.

Zion NPS

Zion, in southwestern Utah, had been a national park for 11 years when this picture was taken in 1930. This incomparable span is the 156-foot-long Bridge Mountain Arch.

Prophets

They were planners and pols—and, of course, philosophers, too, like graybeards John Burroughs and John Muir, trading views during their walks together. They were visionaries one and all, who carried the day because they made sense. One of the most influential, Theodore Roosevelt, expressed it succinctly: "There is nothing more practical than the preservation of beauty."

t started in the 19th century, not as a political crusade or any kind of organized environmental movement, but rather as a floating idea, a notion held in common by a philosopher here, a poet there, an urban landscape architect, a rural landscape painter, a hiker, an explorer. It was often posed as a question: Is there perhaps a reason to resist our human instinct to develop this pristine place? Mightn't it be prudent to conserve this scenery, this wilderness, these flora and fauna? Do our offspring and theirs have a right to behold and enjoy this splendor as we do today? Are we less or more harmonious with our maker if we choose preservation over industry? Is it possible—is it, perchance, our duty—to sanctify the most magnificent natural gifts that we have been bequeathed?

As the notion evolved, it attracted adherents among commonfolk and, eventually, bureaucrats and politicians, including a few United States Presidents (T.R. principal among them). When it at

George Catlin

In 1832, the year he arrived in the Dakotas, Catlin painted the Missouri River (below) and dreamed of a national park there. Today, there is one.

last coalesced and was formalized by various acts of Congress, the notion had become an initiative wholly original anywhere on the planet. Yes, Olde England had its centuries-long parade of pastoralists, and treks had been taken into the majestic mountains of Asia, Africa and South America since time immemorial. But no one before had thought of treating nature in quite this way: institutionally setting it aside, to be protected for its own sake and that of generations to come.

The theory that led to the establishment of the first national park, in 1872, thence to the National Park Service more than half a century later, has no single father, no Einstein or Edison. Yet the claim can be made that the artist George Catlin was the first to conjure a large national wilderness park in the American West. Catlin arrived in the Dakotas in 1832 to record the life of Indians inhabiting the region. So taken was he with the scenery that he wondered if it might be possible to establish "by some great protecting policy of govern-

somewhat as beautiful as his own nature." Emerson was writing in an age when the American horizon usually inspired expansionist yearnings, and one contemporaneous critic predicted that many of *Nature*'s readers would dismiss it as "mere moonshine." But the young philosopher from Massachusetts was on to something.

As was his friend and townsman from Concord, Henry David Thoreau, the naturalist who would write over two million words in his short, 44-year life, inspiring countless millions to live more simply and self-reliantly. The ideas in many of his books and essays—*Walden*, "Civil Disobedience," "Walking"—were revolutionary and can now be seen as remarkably prescient. Certainly his formula for preservation of wilderness as outlined in his essay "Huckleberries" was both. In analyzing the state of affairs in and around his hometown, Thoreau suggested that every village should set aside "a primitive forest . . . where a stick should never be cut for fuel . . . but stand and decay for higher uses—a common possession for-

ment . . . [a] nation's park, containing man and beast, in all the wild and freshness of their nature's beauty." While Catlin's proposition seems a blueprint for what eventually came to pass, it should be noted that others had already been arguing against overbuilding in scenic areas. Development near Niagara Falls had been ongoing since 1806, and critics pointed to that despoilment as Exhibit A for What Not to Do. And in 1832, the very same year that Catlin planted his easel in the West, Congress declared the Hot Springs Reservation in Arkansas—today, Hot Springs National Park—off-limits to developers.

In September 1836, thirty-three-year-old Ralph Waldo Emerson anonymously published a pamphlet, what he called his "little azure-coloured *Nature*." An argument for values inherent in the natural order, the essay claimed that nature's "enchantments are medicinal, they sober and heal us" and that "Nature never wears a mean appearance . . . In the tranquil landscape, and especially in the distant line of the horizon, man beholds

Henry David Thoreau

His hypothesis, which held that communities should dedicate a portion of land to wilderness, is now the guiding principle behind parks national, state, rural and urban.

Ralph Waldo Emerson

He was in concord with friend Thoreau in their regard for Nature, cap N, but approached the subject more abstractly, through poetry and philosophy but never polemic.

Human Action in 1864. The book, whose working title had been *Man the Disturber of Nature's Harmonies,* was famously called by Lewis Mumford "the fountainhead of the conservation movement." In this groundbreaking discourse on environmental degradation, Marsh chronicled how, since ancient Rome, "Man's ignorant disregard of the laws of nature" had been responsible for regular, sometimes irreparable ecological harm. Natural decay was due to geological causes "whose action we can neither resist or guide," as well as to "the direct violence of hostile human force." The same year that Marsh was issuing his well-argued polemic in Europe, the American President back home, hearing a small but swelling cry in the land against wanton degradation, signed a federal authorization that gave awesome Yosemite Valley and the stunning Mariposa grove of sequoia trees to California for "public use, resort and recreation." So, before the United States had a national park, none other than Abraham Lincoln, a crusader in so many things, formalized the establishment of the first state park.

Yosemite, in its park infancy, enticed several notable characters, some of whose fates were formed by Yosemite, some who helped shape Yosemite's fate. The landscape architect Frederick Law Olmsted was appointed the first chairman of Yosemite's board of commissioners, and it was his 1865 report that offered views not only on how Yosemite should be set up but how other big parks might look and function. Olmsted, born in 1822

ever." He posited each town's preserved wilderness at approximately a mile square, which circa 1850 would have represented about 3.8 percent of Concord's area. Today, the national parks, all 83.3 million acres of them, constitute .35 percent of the United States landmass.

Others followed in the footprints of Emerson and Thoreau. John Burroughs, born on a farm in the Catskills, became a preeminent outdoors writer, a poetic champion of wild places: "We go to nature for solitude and for communion with our souls . . . One's own landscape comes in time to be a sort of outlying part of himself . . . cut those trees, and he bleeds; mar those hills, he suffers." Henry James found Burroughs "a more humorous, more available and more sociable Thoreau." John Muir would find him an inspiration and boon hiking companion—but we'll get to that.

George Perkins Marsh, born to privilege in Vermont, was on appointment as President Lincoln's minister to Italy when he published *Man and Nature: Or, Physical Geography as Modified by*

George Perkins Marsh

The public man from New England was an early Rachel Carson, marshaling science and the observation of historical trends in a fierce, even frantic call for conservation.

Frederick Law Olmsted

As opposed to his contemporary Marsh, Olmsted wasn't above working with nature—molding it, improving upon it—to make it yet more pleasurable to man.

in Hartford and raised as a gentleman, was already an urban legend for his work on green-space designs in New York City, most notably Central Park. He brought to his California appointment the same vision he would bring to later projects in Chicago, Boston and Montreal: a desire to improve and prettify things, and to make public spaces a haven for recreation and spiritual replenishment. "Tranquility and rest to the mind" was his grail in shaping a setting, "the greatest possible contrast with the restraining and confining condition of the town." But Olmsted, indisputably the foremost landscape architect of the 19th century, was never hands-off, even in a place as naturally grandiose as Yosemite, where he

Teddy Roosevelt and John Muir
Having had his philosophy shaped by Muir, President Roosevelt was already influencing events when the men posed on Glacier Point in Yosemite in 1903.

urged trails, hotels, restaurants: amenities that would lure people so that people could partake.

Contrast that philosophy with John Muir's. Born in Scotland, Muir arrived in Wisconsin in 1849 at age 11 and spent time there in the backwoods and later in Canada (perhaps to avoid the Civil War draft). In 1867 a machine accident nearly left him blind, and for months he could barely see. Eventually, the sight in one eye returned to normal, and Muir determined that he would dedicate himself to observing and recording the natural world that he had always been fond of. His plans for a global adventure via the Amazon were curtailed by malaria, and after a period of transcontinental wandering he found himself in

1868 in San Francisco. Once he had recovered from his illness, he sought advice from a companion: What should I do next? Muir later recalled, "'But where do you want to go?' asked the man to whom I had applied for this important information. 'To any place that is wild,' I said." He was supplied with directions east, to Yosemite.

There, he worked first as a shepherd, then in a sawmill, then as a guide, one knowledgeable above all others. He led such VIP visitors as Emerson, who told Muir he should leave his post in the outback, take to the podium, and share his attractive philosophy with the masses. Muir, however, demurred. He stayed on the job and showed Burroughs, whom he idolized as he idolized Emerson, some nooks and crannies in and around El Capitan. He guided, and lobbied, the rabid outdoorsman and hunter Teddy Roosevelt. He refined his philosophy and began to write; he became a political figure. His thinking, as explicated in arguments published in Robert Underwood Johnson's *Century* magazine—and as informed by such thinkers as the passionate Burroughs ("Everybody needs beauty as well as bread," Muir wrote in a Burroughs-like way, "places to play in and pray in, where nature may heal and give strength to body and soul")—would lead to the preservation of a larger, all-encompassing tract called Yosemite National Park in 1890, and culminate with the founding of the Sierra Club in 1892.

Meanwhile, in Yellowstone . . .

There had been rumors for much of the 19th century—in fact, since the first white man happened upon the area in 1807—that there were strange and wondrous phenomena ongoing in a vast tract of land straddling the Wyoming and Montana territories. In 1870, Henry Dana Washburn, a former Republican congressman from Indiana and, before that, a general in the Union Army, led an expedition into the mysterious region, hoping to find the headwaters of the Yellowstone River. Washburn and his fellow travelers were not environmentalists by persuasion or philosophy, but they were so impressed by the lakes, valleys and particularly the geysers in the region that they concurred—with but one dissenter—when a member of their team, Montana judge Cornelius Hedges, suggested that the area be preserved as a park. After having returned from their journey,

Yosemite

In 1890, Yosemite's status changed from that of a California state park to that of a national park. The very same year, painter Thomas Hill recorded a vista, with hunters in the right foreground, from a perspective similar to that later employed by Roosevelt and Muir's portraitist.

during which they gave name to Old Faithful, Giant and Giantess among several other blow-holes, the men pushed their referendum with lectures, editorials and articles, arguing not just from a tree-hugger's perspective but from that of a tourist agent. With the enthusiastic support of rail officials and concessionaires, they carried the day, and in 1872, President Ulysses S. Grant signed a bill creating Yellowstone National Park—national, because Wyoming and Montana, unlike California, had not yet achieved statehood and were thus unable to administer the land. The law stipulated that Yellowstone was "for the benefit and enjoyment of all people" and "for the preservation, from injury or spoilation, of all timber, mineral deposits, natural curiosities or wonders." That last word kept appearing in reference to Yellowstone, and the park was dubbed America's Wonderland. It was the first national park anywhere in the world and the physical manifestation of what had been, until that moment, just an idea.

It didn't look like such a terrific idea when Yellowstone opened for business. People did flock to the region, but among them were bison-poachers, timber-cutters and even vandals who desecrated land surrounding the thermal vents. Since the feds were now responsible for the area, there was nothing to do but send in the Army to manage affairs, a condition that held from 1886 to 1916. Others, too, sought to bolster protections in Yellowstone. In 1887, that roughriding native of New York City—Roosevelt again; he appears often in this saga—formed the Boone and Crockett Club with an eye toward helping out in Yellowstone, and in 1894, Congress passed the National Park Protective Act which strengthened conservation rules in the three parks then overseen by the U.S. Interior Department (California's Yosemite and Sequoia had been federalized in 1890).

At one point, alluding specifically to Yellowstone but forwarding his general views concerning the government's responsibility for all protected lands, Roosevelt wrote, "[I]t is a park for the people, and the representatives of the people should see that it is molested in no way." By 1901, when he became President upon the assassination of William McKinley, he was in a position to act forcefully upon his words. During his years in the White House, which lasted until 1909, he signed authorizations doubling the total of national parks from five to 10 and ordered protections for 18 other parcels under the designation National Monuments. (Some of these, such as Arizona's Petrified Forest and Grand Canyon, would later become national parks.) In 1903, by executive order, he established a federally protected wildlife refuge, setting aside Pelican Island in Florida's Indian River; it was only the first of 53 wildlife sanctuaries Roosevelt created as President. T.R. oversaw creation of the U.S. Forest Service and worked with its first administrator, Gifford Pinchot, to roll back the rapid denuding of woodlands coast-to-coast. Roosevelt was the right chief executive at the right time for the conservation movement in America.

Which is not to say that the movement enjoyed clear sailing during his tenure. As but one example concerning the national parks: In 1905 the U.S. Congress, caving to the petitions of mining, logging and grazing interests, reduced the size of Yosemite National Park by 542 square miles. Muir and his confederates were, of course, appalled, and they grew even more concerned when San Francisco started a campaign to claim the waters of the Tuolumne River for its own municipal supply. When the city proposed a dam on the Tuolumne at the mouth of Hetch Hetchy Valley in Yosemite, Muir flew into a fine Scottish passion: "These temple destroyers, devotees of ravaging commercialism, seem to have a perfect contempt for Nature, and, instead of lifting their eyes to the God of the mountains, lift them to the Almighty Dollar.

"Dam Hetch Hetchy! As well dam for watertanks the people's cathedrals and churches, for no holier temple has ever been consecrated by the heart of man." Muir's violent rhetoric fell on deaf ears in Washington, and in 1913, Congress withdrew the valley from the park and gave it to the city. The dam was built, and one of Yosemite's two most spectacular valleys disappeared beneath a lake. "The worst disaster ever to come to any National Park," the historian John Ise called it.

Roosevelt, Muir and a growing army of likeminded conservationists hoped to head off other such transgressions in the parks—but how? In February 1912, private citizen Roosevelt, writing in the same journal, *The Outlook,* where Muir had waged his campaign against the dam, proposed "the establishment of the National Park Service." This was, he said, "justified by considerations of

Henry Dana Washburn

The former Civil War general was surveyor general of the Montana territory when his 1870 expedition spent a month "discovering" Yellowstone. Their reports led to the park's enshrinement.

good administration, of the value of natural beauty as a National asset, and of the effectiveness of outdoor life and recreation in the production of good citizenship." A separate governmental division within the Interior Department, one that was dedicated to nothing else but caring for and caring about the parks, would be better able to fend off threats to the land, Roosevelt and his supporters knew, and would, over time, elevate management that was grossly uneven throughout the unconnected system.

On August 25, 1916, President Woodrow Wilson signed legislation creating the National Park Service, whose charge was to oversee Interior's parks, monuments and "such other national parks and reservations of like character as may be hereafter created by Congress." To date, the hereafter has seen the Park Service's various protected areas

Yellowstone

In 1872, the year that Yellowstone was decreed the world's first national park by President Grant, the artist Thomas Moran depicted the Grand Canyon of the Yellowstone River. The area's new status attracted more visitors—and more problems.

increase in number to 388, in nearly every state and U.S. possession—of which the grandest glories, America's so-called Crown Jewels, are the 55 national parks.

Several people, from Roosevelt's contemporary James Bryce, who was Great Britain's ambassador to the United States, to the great writer of the American West, Wallace Stegner, have called the national parks America's best-ever idea. They're right, of course, but in another way wrong. Ideas don't come from countries, they come from the minds—and hearts—of men. George Catlin. Ralph Waldo Emerson. Henry David Thoreau. George Perkins Marsh and John Burroughs. Frederick Law Olmsted. Henry Dana Washburn and Cornelius Hedges. John Muir. Teddy Roosevelt. They shared a notion about the land, and willed the notion to reality.

The Great Parks

In the superb treasure chest belonging to the National Park Service there are nearly 400 holdings, including National Recreation Areas, National Monuments, National Historic Sites and other designations. But the pride of the collection is the 55 National Parks (56 if you separate the conjoined Sequoia and King's Canyon). These are the ones called "the great parks" or, more poetically, America's Crown Jewels. Those east of the Continental Divide are indicated on this satellite photo, and the western parks, including those in Alaska and Hawaii, are indexed on the following two pages. The information for parks in American Samoa and the Virgin Islands is below.

National Park of American Samoa
Superintendent
Pago Pago, AS 96799
011-684-633-7082
www.nps.gov/npsa

Virgin Islands National Park
1300 Cruz Bay Creek
St. John, VI 00830
340-776-6201
www.nps.gov/viis

Satellite composites by Tom Van Sant and The GeoSphere Project

7 Guadalupe Mountains National Park
H.C. 60, Box 400
Salt Flat, TX 79847
915-828-3251
www.nps.gov/gumo

8 Big Bend National Park
P.O. Box 129
Big Bend National Park, TX 79834
915-477-2251
www.nps.gov/bibe

9 Hot Springs National Park
P.O. Box 1860
Hot Springs, AR 71902
501-624-2701
www.nps.gov/hosp

10 Mammoth Cave National Park
P.O. Box 7
Mammoth Cave, KY 42259
270-758-2251
www.nps.gov/maca

11 Great Smoky Mountains National Park
107 Park Headquarters Rd.
Gatlinburg, TN 37738
865-436-1200
www.nps.gov/grsm

12 Cuyahoga Valley National Park
15610 Vaughn Rd.
Brecksville, OH 44141
216-524-1497
www.nps.gov/cuva

13 Shenandoah National Park
3655 U.S. Hwy. 211 East
Luray, VA 22835
540-999-3500
www.nps.gov/shen

14 Acadia National Park
P.O. Box 177
Eagle Lake Rd.
Bar Harbor, ME 04609
207-288-3338
www.nps.gov/acad

15 Dry Tortugas National Park
P.O. Box 6208
Key West, FL 33041
305-242-7700
www.nps.gov/drto

16 Everglades National Park
40001 State Road 9336
Homestead, FL 33034
305-242-7700
www.nps.gov/ever

17 Biscayne National Park
9700 SW 328 St.
Homestead, FL 33033
305-230-7275
www.nps.gov/bisc

3 Badlands National Park
P.O. Box 6
Interior, SD 57750
605-433-5361
www.nps.gov/badl

4 Voyageurs National Park
3131 Hwy. 53 South
International Falls, MN 56649
218-283-9821
www.nps.gov/voya

5 Isle Royale National Park
800 E. Lakeshore Dr.
Houghton, MI 49931
906-482-0984
www.nps.gov/isro

6 Carlsbad Caverns National Park
3225 National Parks Hwy.
Carlsbad, NM 88220
505-785-2232
www.nps.gov/cave

1 Theodore Roosevelt National Park
P.O. Box 7
Medora, ND 58645
701-623-4466
www.nps.gov/thro

2 Wind Cave National Park
R.R. 1 Box 190
Hot Springs, SD 57747
605-745-4600
www.nps.gov/wica

1 Olympic National Park
600 East Park Ave.
Port Angeles, WA 98362
360-565-3130
www.nps.gov/olym

2 North Cascades National Park
810 State Rte. 20
Sedro-Woolley,
WA 98284
360-856-5700
www.nps.gov/noca

3 Mount Rainier National Park
Tahoma Woods, Star Rte.
Ashford, WA 98304
360-569-2211 ext. 3314
www.nps.gov/mora

4 Crater Lake National Park
P.O. Box 7
Crater Lake, OR 97604
541-594-3100
www.nps.gov/crla

5 Redwood National & State Parks
1111 Second St.
Crescent City, CA 95531
707-464-6101
www.nps.gov/redw

6 Lassen Volcanic National Park
P.O. Box 100
Mineral, CA 96063
530-595-4444
www.nps.gov/lavo

7 Yosemite National Park
P.O. Box 577
Yosemite National Park,
CA 95389
209-372-0200
www.nps.gov/yose

8 Sequoia & Kings Canyon National Parks
47050 Generals Hwy.
Three Rivers, CA 93271
559-565-3341
www.nps.gov/seki

9 Death Valley National Park
P.O. Box 579
Death Valley, CA 92328
760-786-3200
www.nps.gov/deva

10 Channel Islands National Park
1901 Spinnaker Dr.
Ventura, CA 93001
805-658-5711
www.nps.gov/chis

11 Joshua Tree National Park
74485 National Park Dr.
Twentynine Palms,
CA 92277
760-367-5500
www.nps.gov/jotr

12 Saguaro National Park
3693 South Old
Spanish Trail
Tucson, AZ 85730
520-733-5100
www.nps.gov/sagu

13 Petrified Forest National Park
P.O. Box 2217
Petrified Forest National
Park, AZ 86028
928-524-6228
www.nps.gov/pefo

14 Grand Canyon National Park
P.O. Box 129
Grand Canyon,
AZ 86023
928-638-7888
www.nps.gov/grca

15 Great Basin National Park
100 Great Basin
National Park
Baker, NV 89311
775-234-7331
www.nps.gov/grba

16 Zion National Park
S.R. 9
Springdale,
UT 84767
435-772-3256
www.nps.gov/zion

17 Bryce Canyon National Park
P.O. Box 170001
Bryce Canyon,
UT 84717
435-834-5322
www.nps.gov/brca

18 Capitol Reef National Park
H.C. 70, Box 15
Torrey, UT 84775
435-425-3791
www.nps.gov/care

19 Canyonlands National Park
2282 South West
Resource Blvd.
Moab, UT 84532
435-719-2313
www.nps.gov/cany

20 Arches National Park
P.O. Box 907
Moab, UT 84532
435-719-2299
www.nps.gov/arch

21 Mesa Verde National Park
P.O. Box 8
Mesa Verde National
Park, CO 81330
970-529-4465
www.nps.gov/meve

22 Black Canyon of the Gunnison National Park
Park Headquarters
102 Elk Creek
Gunnison, CO 81230
970-641-2337
www.nps.gov/blca

23 Rocky Mountain National Park
1000 Hwy. 36
Estes Park, CO 80517
970-586-1206
www.nps.gov/romo

Alaska and Hawaii

27 Kobuk Valley National Park
P.O. Box 1029
Kotzebue, AK 99752
907-442-3890
www.nps.gov/kova

28 Gates of the Arctic National Park & Preserve
Bettles Ranger Station (Field Ops)
P.O. Box 26030
Bettles, AK 99726
907-692-5494
www.nps.gov/gaar

29 Katmai National Park & Preserve
P.O. Box 7, #1 King Salmon Mall
King Salmon, AK 99613
907-246-3305
www.nps.gov/katm

30 Lake Clark National Park & Preserve
4230 University Dr.
Ste. 311
Anchorage, AK 99508
907-781-2218
www.nps.gov/lacl

31 Kenai Fjords National Park
National Park Service
P.O. Box 1727
Seward, AK 99664
907-224-3175
www.nps.gov/kefj

32 Denali National Park & Preserve
P.O. Box 9
Denali Park, AK 99755
907-683-2294
www.nps.gov/dena

33 Wrangell–St. Elias National Park & Preserve
106.8 Richardson Hwy.
P.O. Box 439
Copper Center, AK 99573
907-822-5234
www.nps.gov/wrst

34 Glacier Bay National Park & Preserve
P.O. Box 140
Gustavus, AK 99826
907-697-2230
www.nps.gov/glba

35 Haleakala National Park
P.O. Box 369
Makawao, Maui, HI 96768
808-572-4400
www.nps.gov/hale

36 Hawaii Volcanoes National Park
P.O. Box 52
Hawaii National Park, HI 96718
808-985-6000
www.nps.gov/havo

24 Grand Teton National Park
P.O. Drawer 170
Moose, WY 83012
307-739-3300
www.nps.gov/grte

25 Yellowstone National Park
P.O. Box 168
Yellowstone National Park, WY 82190
307-344-7381
www.nps.gov/yell

26 Glacier National Park
Park Headquarters
West Glacier, MT 59936
406-888-7800
www.nps.gov/glac

Lower Falls glistens as early morning sunshine creeps into the Grand Canyon of the Yellowstone River. The river was what lured explorers to the region, where they found many other—and far stranger—natural wonders.

1872–1890

The First Parks

In Yellowstone, Yosemite and Sequoia, an idea took root.

Previous pages: Jeff Gnass

Today, more than 100 countries throughout the world have national parks or reserves, but in 1870, when Congress created a park at the headwaters of the Yellowstone River, there was only one. No one was certain what a national park was. Yellowstone would be an experiment—as would the two other great parks that followed in 1890, California's Yosemite and Sequoia.

From the first, ingredients in the national park formula included the idea of publicly held land, a respect for wildlife, and Frederick Law Olmsted's take on leisure—mankind's need for respite from what was even then considered "the modern world." But how much weight each of these would carry in the equation wasn't stipulated, so how to balance them was anyone's guess. The railroad

companies built huge hotels in the early parks, and development was uneven at best. There was no call for hunting to disappear when a park was designated, nor was forestry or exploitation of other natural resources ruled out. It was believed back East that whatever land was being set aside left of the Mississippi might be scenic but was otherwise useless. When it was found that this was not the case, that there might exist subsurface or other energy potential, rules and sometimes boundaries were redrawn.

Then came the automobile. In 1912, James Bryce, Britain's ambassador to the U.S. and one of the first to recognize the spiritual value of America's parks, weighed in on whether to admit cars into Yosemite Valley: "There are plenty of roads everywhere for lovers of speed and noise, without intruding on these few places where the wood

A New Clientele

Within a decade of Yellowstone's designation as the world's first national park, these ladies from the East pose on its limestone terraces. As hunters and trappers were joined in the still-wild West by tourists, brand-new pressures were brought to bear upon the land.

Early Errors

In making access to the parks easier for gentlefolk, many mistakes were made, such as carving a thoroughfare through a giant sequoia in Yosemite's Mariposa grove. The bears of Yellowstone took to cars more happily than did conservationists, as cars meant lunch.

nymphs and the water nymphs ought to be allowed to remain in untroubled seclusion, and their true worshipers to have the landscape to themselves."

In the event, the nymphs have never been left alone. As proponents of the first three parks

learned, gaining protection as parkland did not lessen but formalized an area's status as an arena of controversy. Over time, laws and the will of the people have given conservationists an edge in the parks, but only an edge. Everyone has seen antique postcards of jalopies being driven through redwood trees, and in 1935 California's very first ski area, Badger Pass, opened in Yosemite (this past winter, snow tubing debuted at Badger). Consider tensions in the original park: Yellowstone today, which covers 3,472 square miles, has 950 miles of trails but also 466 miles of roads. In 1995 wolves, hunted for decades, were reintroduced into the park. In November 2002, even as the National Park Service was concluding an internal report that said banning snowmobiles was the best way to protect the park's air quality and wildlife, the Bush administration reopened Yellowstone and Grand Teton to the vehicles.

The push and pull seems eternal, yet national parks have found their place in the country's fabric through trial, error and compromise. The magnificence that has been retained in the oldest parks proves that the fight is always worth fighting.

An Eerie Yellowstone

The park sits atop a 2000° lake of molten rock, an underground pressure cooker 50 miles long and 30 wide. For at least a few million years, since magma burned a hole under ancient Wyoming's bedrock, Yellowstone periodically disgorged a small ocean of lava in eruptions hundreds of times worse than any recent volcanic explosion on earth. Today, volcanic action heats rock below the surface, and this in turn creates all manner of thermal spectacle in thousands of steaming hot springs and hundreds of geysers, plus bubbling mudpots and fumaroles. At Mammoth Hot Springs, water wells up, carrying with it dissolved minerals that form an elegant limestone staircase (right).

Michael Melford

Life in a Strange Land

In 1894, with human predators continuing to stalk wildlife within park boundaries, Congress passed the National Park Protective Act to "protect the birds and animals in Yellowstone National Park." Today, 3,600 bison roam throughout Yellowstone; the pair above forage on an island in the Firehole River. There are hundreds of bears in Yellowstone, and the recent reintroduction of wolves has been successful. Left: The park's most famous geyser, Old Faithful, erupts every 88 minutes. Opposite: The heated water in the many basins allow vivid blue, yellow and green microbes to grow year-round.

Thrilling Yosemite

While all views in Yosemite National Park are spectacular, some take pride of place. From many points in the Sierras, 10,880-foot Unicorn Peak, seen reflected in a high-country pond, is a distinctive landmark. To the southwest is Glacier Point, perhaps the most famous vantage in the West. From atop the cliff a visitor beholds waterfalls, distant mountains and neighboring Half Dome. In 1962 park officials staged a firefall for the amusement of tourists, but, in truth, no stunt or embellishment is necessary to make Yosemite's natural attributes glow.

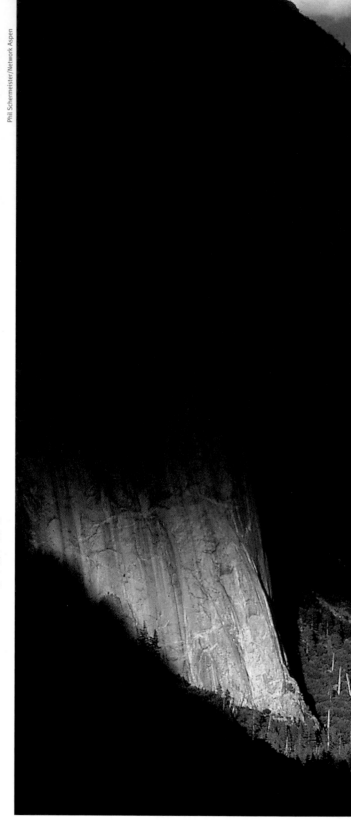

Grace and Grandeur

John Muir, upon viewing the Sierra Nevada, declared it a Range of Light. Indeed, there are everywhere dramatic shadows and vibrant slashes of sunshine—deep greens, brilliant yellows and stark grays intermixing. Left: A stoic juniper tree fighting its way through granite makes for a poignant photographic study, while a trio of Sierra peaks—Mount Dana (13,053 feet, second highest in Yosemite), Mount Gibbs (12,764) and Mammoth Peak (12,016)—support Muir's vision. There are trails to the top of all three, as there are to the summit of Yosemite's most famous formation, Half Dome, seen above at right. Half of its 8,842 feet of altitude rises straight from the valley floor.

Surprising Sequoia

The name of Sequoia National Park belies the variety of terrain and vegetation lying therein; it's not just about big trees. After being blended with neighboring Kings Canyon National Park in 1940, what was originally designated a 50,000-acre forest sanctuary in 1890 had grown to encompass more than 1,300 square miles of mountains, waterways and wildlife refuge that could rival those of its California cousin, Yosemite. Set on the western flank of the Sierra Nevada Range, Sequoia rises from the mild to the magnificent. In the foothills, buckeyes and oaks enjoy a spring greening as, on high, Hamilton Creek froths.

Fred Hirschmann

Carr Clifton/Minden Pictures

Rugged Rock, Tallest of Trees

From 1,500 to 4,500 feet there are oak and chaparral,
and even a few yucca plants. In Sequoia's mid-elevations,
ranging to 9,000 feet, are meadows, conifers and the
giant sequoias, deemed by Muir "the most beautiful
and majestic" trees on the planet. Higher up are the
formidable peaks of the Great Western Divide and the
Sierra Crest, topping out at over 13,000 feet and yielding,
finally, to the domain of Mount Whitney, apex of the
Lower 48 at 14,494 feet. Black bears, coyotes and gray
foxes work the range, while alpine flora—yellow blazing
stars, Indian paintbrushes—add color, brightening the
harsher, higher places. Above: granite that long ago was
polished by glaciers. Right: a stand of lodgepole pines.

Linda Bartlett/Folio Inc.

David Sanger

John Skowronski/Folio Inc.

Urban Preserves

Well before the U.S. protected the wilderness in its first national parks, other governments big and small had set aside land whose serenity might provide relief to the citizenry. Ancient Rome had its prettified piazzas, and Dickensian London its splendid parks and gardens (not all public). Even in America, the establishment of urban sanctuaries as oases in a world of hustle and bustle predated the national parks, and most of the old preserves are intact today, variously administered by municipal, state or federal authorities, and supported by tax dollars, private trusts and Friends of the Park. From 1850 to 1900, the thinking behind city parks was to create "pleasure gardens" to which an urbanite could escape. The idea's champion—both its Philosopher King and hands-on architect—was Frederick Law Olmsted. He felt that

2,000 airy, designed acres were needed to ameliorate stresses inherent in a good-size metropolis, and did his best for the people of New York, Boston, Baltimore and other cities. In the 20th century, playgrounds were added to the mix, then came the concept of pristine open space. No place better illustrates the value and variety of urban preserves than San Francisco, down by the Bay (above). Golden Gate Park, administered by the city, draws 75,000 on a weekend to its walkways, arboretum, dog runs and basketball courts, while the Golden Gate National Recreation Area, the world's largest urban park and part of the federal Park Service, has some 75,398 acres, including 28 miles of coastline, within its boundaries. The Muir Woods National Monument is part of Golden Gate, and so is Alcatraz. Opposite: In the nation's capital, Rock Creek Park (top) is, suitably, part of the Park Service, as is the C&O Canal National Historic Park, which wends its way from Georgetown to Cumberland, Md.

The Pioneering William Henry Jackson

When evidence was needed that this land was worth preserving, his pictures spoke a thousand words.

While Emerson, Thoreau, Burroughs, Marsh and Co. were influential in assembling a philosophical foundation that might underlay the parks, it was another artist from back East whose suasion was more empirical. In fact, it would be remiss not to state that the photographs of William Henry Jackson of Keeseville, N.Y., had a direct impact on the establishment of the world's first national park.

The daguerreotype process was born in 1839, Jackson four years later. By age 15 he was working in the nascent art form as a retoucher. When the Civil War interrupted in 1861, Jackson served the Union, most often on garrison duty. The war ended, and not long thereafter Jackson listened to a siren's song coming from the wild West. He

A Hard-working Man in the High Country

In order to capture panoramas such as the Lower Falls of the Yellowstone (opposite), Jackson would lug his substantial gear to the highest possible elevations. Above: The artist uncaps the lens—and holds his breath—on Glacier Point in Yosemite. Left: In Utah, Jackson inspects the results of work just completed in his "dark tent."

headed for the Nebraska Territory in 1866. He worked briefly as a bullwhacker, wandered the Oregon Trail, then opened a photographic studio in Omaha in 1867.

Photography was extremely difficult in those days. Collodion-coated glass negatives were state of the art, but they were bulky, gooey, cumbersome, altogether dicey, propositions. "Viewing," said Jackson of photography, "meant labor, patience and moral stamina." He himself "prayed every time the lens was uncapped."

Drawn to the outdoors, he did his uncapping in inhospitable places. Beginning in 1869, he photographed the new Union Pacific Railroad line. With his portable "dark tent," cameras and glass negatives—photos could not yet be enlarged, so

Days at the Office

Jackson's commissions with Hayden's survey of Yellowstone and with the railroads produced stunning art along with evidence for easterners that Old Faithful was the real thing and that transport through the Rockies was available, if harrowing.

Men and Mountains
Whether in Utah's Uintas (above) or Colorado's Rockies (opposite, bottom), Jackson would include a figure to add scale.

negs were massive—Jackson was hauling 300 pounds of equipment to the site. "I have made a negative in 15 minutes," he reported, "from the time the first rope was thrown from the pack to the final repacking. Ordinarily, however, half an hour was little enough time to do the work."

Ferdinand Hayden, who was organizing an exploration of the Yellowstone region in the wake of Henry Dana Washburn's dispatches from there, learned of Jackson and asked him to come along as a documentarian. Washburn's reports were subsequently presented to Congress, but it wasn't until legislators were given portfolios of Jackson's fantastic photographs that the acclamation was

Library of Congress (top); George Eastman House

general: This land must be protected.

Jackson continued to shoot the West, including many locales that are now within park boundaries. He lived to a good old age—he was 99 when he died in New York City in 1942—and always remained self-effacing about his contributions to the nation's natural history. In his autobiography, Jackson recalled that there was another professional photographer who had recorded Yellowstone at about the same time he had, but that the other guy's work had been lost in Chicago's Great Fire of 1871. "That my pictures were the only ones published," wrote Jackson, "is something for which I have to thank Mrs. O'Leary's cow."

True to Life

Jackson mastered a process that yielded hand-tinted, mass-produced postcards of scenes like Yosemite (top), which sold big.

When a volcano blew the top off a mountain in the Cascades, snowmelt and rain filled the resultant cavity to form Crater Lake—at 1,932 feet the deepest water in the country. Here, the island Phantom Ship rises amidst 21 square miles of the bluest of waters.

1902–1915

Second Generation

Progress was slow until Teddy Roosevelt led the charge.

Previous pages: Jeff Gnass

By 1890 the first three national parks had been beatified, but becoming clearer with every passing year was the fact that, as Calvin Coolidge would put it a quarter century later, America's business was business. Thus while John Muir might recognize that "the clearest way into the universe is through a forest wilderness," there were others just as fervent who espied a different pathway to heaven. Where Muir saw fruitful woodland and hallowed ground, there were those who, with an equally and increasingly appreciative eye, saw timber and mineral deposits. Pressure from factions seeking to make a profit from national park areas became—and would continue to be—as much a part of the scene as the sequoia. The protectors, though, shared Goethe's sentiments: "Nature is beneficent. I praise

An Ancient Land . . .

The explorer George Bird Grinnell pushed to get Glacier the status of a national park. Here, Indians camp on the 10-mile-long St. Mary Lake in 1912. There is evidence of people—perhaps ancestors of today's resident tribes—using these lands more than 10,000 years ago.

her and all her works. She is silent and wise. She is cunning, but for good ends. She has brought me here and will also lead me away . . . I trust her." But the protectors had enemies, and battles to be fought.

As the 19th century neared its end, the nation was urbanizing in response to torrents of immigrants, and the eradication of nature was irrupting in consequence. The effort to enisle the parks, to create profoundly timeless preserves offering unimpaired respite from pollution of every form, became a struggle. And the protectors well and truly struggled. While differences of opinion regarding the sanctity of nature might have hobbled certain preservations, an almost complete lack of unified tactics, let alone strategy, was the real culprit. The conservationists were dealing, after all, with not only virgin land but also

44 **LIFE** SECOND GENERATION

on Country Life, which addressed growing apprehension about the diminution of rural areas. These and many other actions drove wilderness concerns to the forefront, and prompted the establishment of more and more parks—more kinds of parks, in different kinds of places—including South Dakota's Wind Cave (1903), Colorado's Mesa Verde (1906), Montana's Glacier (1910), Colorado's Rocky Mountain (1915) and two that encompassed volcanic land: Hawaii and California's Lassen, both in 1916. Bernard De Voto portrayed well this need to preserve: "It is imperative to maintain portions of the wilderness untouched so that . . . moderns may at least see what their ancestors knew in their nerves and blood."

. . . Lands of Surprise and Awe

For some, like Teddy Roosevelt (at right, saluting the Rocky Mountains in 1905), the national parks were a home away from home. For others, the wild out-of-doors was a complete novelty. Above, visitors to Hawaii's Kilauea toast postcards over cracks in the active volcano's hardened lava.

uncharted waters. Yes, they had set aside a few parks—but how to keep the ball rolling? There was no effective plan, and consequently Washington's Mount Rainier wasn't deemed a national park until 1899—nine years after Yosemite and Sequoia. Still three more years passed before Crater Lake in Oregon became the first park of the 20th century.

Then things picked up steam. Having a man like T.R. at the helm during the formative years was of inestimable importance. In 1903, with Pelican Island in Florida, he created his first of dozens of federally protected wildlife refuges. That same year, in response to acrimonious debate over the administration of public land in the West, the steady chief executive appointed a commission to study the difficult question of grazing leases for cattlemen. Teddy was outraged at the plundering of southwestern sites, from Spanish missions to ancient pueblos, and in 1906, Congress passed the Antiquities Act, giving the President the power to preserve historic and scenic treasures by declaring them monuments. This authority has figured in a full quarter of all present National Park Service holdings.

In '08, Roosevelt appointed the Commission

Majestic Mount Rainier

The undisputed focal point of the country's fifth-oldest national park is also the fifth-tallest peak in the Lower 48: Mount Rainier, a classic stand-alone pinnacle whose ice cap on a clear day dominates the Seattle skies. Its name was born in 1792 when British explorer Capt. George Vancouver, in the fashion of the time, called it after his friend Rear Adm. Peter Rainier. The massive mountain, adorned with 25 active glaciers, accounts for more than a quarter of the park's 378 square miles. The lower areas are famous for radiant wildflower displays. For a long time, Rainier was regarded as a dormant volcano. Now, however, studies suggest that the old cone may once again breathe fire.

Art Wolfe

Resonant Mesa Verde, Luminous Glacier

When Mesa Verde became a national park in 1906, it marked the first time that a human settlement was so designated. These dwellings in Colorado's Montezuma Valley were built by the Anasazi, ancestral Puebloans who were the Athenians of the Southwest and lived in these 2,000-foot-high abodes during the 13th century, only to vanish mysteriously. Opposite, a view across Grinnell Lake in Glacier suggests the alpine environment that has led to the park's being called the Crown of the Continent; Native Americans knew it as the Backbone of the World. In 1932, Montana's Glacier and Canada's Waterton Lakes were "united" as an international peace park, later designated a World Heritage Site as well.

Fred Hirschmann

Art Wolfe

Regal Rocky Mountain

This is a park of many environments, many life-forms, many different worlds. In the heart of the Rockies stands this Colorado wildness of 416 square miles that boasts more than a hundred peaks surpassing 10,000 feet, bedecked with names like Isolation and Mummy, Chiefs Head and Storm. Some 150 lakes are spread across pastoral and sylvan settings, or found higher up, where they lie frozen for much of the year. Indeed, a quarter of the park extends above the treeline, in wind-raked ecosystems that are home to flora that also inhabit the Arctic. Rocky Mountain, in the words of naturalist Enos Mills, who was tireless in pressing for its national park status, brings "mountain scenes which stir one's blood and which strengthen and sweeten life."

Art Wolfe

Hawaii Volcanoes: Heaven and Hell

It comes as little surprise that a state of such transcendent beauty would be the site for one of America's most thrilling national parks. Hawaii Volcanoes, on the Big Island of Hawaii, is a mesmerizing mosaic of two of the world's most active volcanoes (Kilauea and Mauna Loa), a dense tropical rainforest and thousands of living things that are found nowhere else on earth. It is regrettable that introduced animals— feral pigs, mongooses, cats and dogs—and 900 plants have, in essence, assaulted many native species. Here, molten lava from Kilauea cascades into the sea.

Gregory G. Dimijian/Photo Researchers

Jeff Gnass

When Nature Has Her Way

A hardy native *Sadleria* fern shares the landscape with an army of crusty black monoliths that constitute part of a forest of "lava trees," an interesting by-product of volcanic flow. When the hot lava touched a cool, damp tree—volcanologists call this "quenching"—an insular layer formed that protected the tree until it was, finally, incinerated by the 2000° molten rock. When the lava drained off, the lava tree remained. The top of a "tree" can be several yards high and indicates the height of the lava flow. These remnants may be found in several areas of Hawaii Volcanoes. Opposite: The Holei Sea Arch, where Kilauea meets the Pacific, was created by the collision of water, rock and time.

Wildlife Refuges

In March 2003, the National Wildlife Refuge System launched a centennial celebration marking Theodore Roosevelt's creation of the first NWR (on Pelican Island in Florida). That initial set-aside of 5.5 acres was the progenitor of today's national system, which governs 540 refuges and 3,000 waterfowl production areas on 95 million acres. In 50 states, sanctuary is provided for 700 species of birds and 220 different kinds of mammals, for 250 reptile and amphibian varieties and 200 sorts of fish. Every year, 37 million people enter national refuges. Many of these visitors are children, gaining vital exposure to new and unfamiliar aspects of their world; others may be photographers, or birders looking to add to their life lists, or just folks yearning for a stroll, perhaps

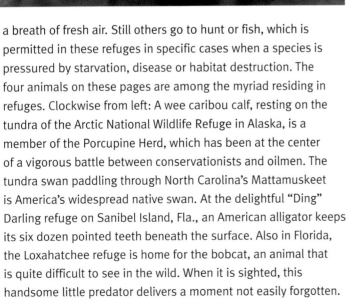

a breath of fresh air. Still others go to hunt or fish, which is permitted in these refuges in specific cases when a species is pressured by starvation, disease or habitat destruction. The four animals on these pages are among the myriad residing in refuges. Clockwise from left: A wee caribou calf, resting on the tundra of the Arctic National Wildlife Refuge in Alaska, is a member of the Porcupine Herd, which has been at the center of a vigorous battle between conservationists and oilmen. The tundra swan paddling through North Carolina's Mattamuskeet is America's widespread native swan. At the delightful "Ding" Darling refuge on Sanibel Island, Fla., an American alligator keeps its six dozen pointed teeth beneath the surface. Also in Florida, the Loxahatchee refuge is home for the bobcat, an animal that is quite difficult to see in the wild. When it is sighted, this handsome little predator delivers a moment not easily forgotten.

Great Smoky Mountains, America's busiest national park, has 270 miles of road for its 10 million annual visitors. But it is on the Quiet Walkways off the asphalt path that these North Carolina and Tennessee hills are best appreciated. Water and hydrocarbons from the dense forest—plus air pollution—provide the haze.

1916–1941
A Formal System

After Years in the Wilderness, a Path to the Future

Granger Collection

Previous pages: Carr Clifton/Minden Pictures

n the wake of Theodore Roosevelt, the nation found itself with all of these national parks. What to do? The answer: Formalize a system, as was finally done with a stroke of Woodrow Wilson's pen on August 25, 1916. The authorization of the National Park Service within the Department of the Interior clarified some things—how a park should be maintained, for example—while leaving certain problems and controversies unre-

solved. In a May 1918 letter to the first U.S. Park Service director, Stephen T. Mather, Interior Secretary Franklin K. Lane said Service policy was based "on three broad principles: First, that the national parks must be maintained in absolutely unimpaired form for the use of future generations as well as those of our own time; second, that they are set apart for the use, observation, health, and pleasure of the people; and third, that the national interest must dictate all decisions affecting pub-

Glorious Horizons

From the rim of Utah's Bryce Canyon, circa 1920, a hiker beholds the great geologic amphitheater and the big sky beyond. Utah National Park, now called Bryce, was authorized in 1924.

Sons of the Pioneers

Landscape architect
Frederick Law Olmsted
worked on California's
Yosemite when it first
became a park, and
decades later his son,
Frederick Jr., helped
design a park on the
other coast: Maine's
Acadia. (At right,
Olmsted *fils* is about
to float his boat in the
waters of Acadia,
the first national park
in the East.) Below:
Explorers led the way
for tourists into the
caverns of Carlsbad,
N.M., which won
park status in 1930.

lic or private enterprise in the parks." The last item had a loophole's aroma, and set the stage for battles to come. Ronald Reagan's inflammatory pro-development Interior Secretary, James G. Watt, saw fit to quote Lane in a 1981 letter to his own Park Service director, Russell E. Dickenson.

From its inception through 1932, the Service was ruled by "Mather men": Stephen, his assistant and successor Horace Albright, and their aids. They wrestled with Lane's principles, then presented a philosophy to the public and Congress. The parks, they felt, were not just for fun and games, but inspiration and education. Mather and associates were of a conservationist bent yet politically prudent, careful not to oppose development in a blanket fashion. They picked battles and won landmark decisions. When the 1920 Federal Power Act authorized dams on public lands, friends of the parks flew into action. In 1921, Congress amended the law to forbid dam-building in national parks and monuments without its specific approval. As to how to approach the signal issue of development, the parks' superintendents passed a resolution rejecting "overdevelopment"—an undefined term whose meaning was clear.

New holdings were added. In 1919 the idea of a national park as a Western tract vanished when Congress set aside part of the Maine coast; the park would later be named Acadia. Grand Canyon's status was upgraded to park in '19, as was that of Utah's Zion. In the '20s: Hot Springs in Arkansas, Bryce Canyon in Utah, Grand Teton in Wyoming. In the 1930s, Shenandoah and Great Smoky Mountains in the South, as well as Carlsbad Caverns in New Mexico and Olympic in Washington, became parks.

A second Roosevelt—Franklin—had a positive if indirect impact on the parks, as his New Deal programs improved tourism infrastructure nationwide, even as people had no money for tourism. In 1940, Isle Royale in Michigan became the first Midwestern park, and the next year Mammoth Cave in Kentucky became the fourth Eastern one.

And then the country went to war. America's gaze, and energy, turned to the fight abroad.

Dazzling Zion

This park's name is entirely apt, as it is taken from a word that may be interpreted as "utopia" or "sanctuary." Zion National Park is a destination of the spirit, a getaway of canyons and plateaus, of domes, waterfalls and elaborate gullies. Sandstone cliffs soar to 3,000 feet while, below, the Virgin River pursues its endless quest amid hanging gardens of columbine. Visitors to Zion are stunned by the dizzying vortex of colors and the striations on rock that have created such wonders as Checkerboard Mesa and Double Arch Alcove. The park's location at the junction of various geographies assures an immense variety of plants and animals. Here, the famed Watchman rises over all.

Tim Fitzharris/Minden Pictures

Carr Clifton/Minden Pictures

Acadia: Atlantic Coast

Park-building in the years leading up to World War I lingered in the majestic sizings of the West, then Maine's Acadia became the only national park east of the Mississippi and would remain so until 1934. Glacier-massaged granite defines the park, lending a robustness to shoreline and contrast to pointy stands of evergreens. At right, a red fox keeps a sly eye out for prey or predator.

Fred Hirschmann

Tim Fitzharris/Minden Pictures

Galen Rowell/Mountain Light

The Grand Grand Canyon

The evolution of Arizona's Grand Canyon commenced two billion years ago when tectonic mayhem, water, erosion and deposition (the formation of rock from various materials) converged symphonically. Then 60 million years ago, two geologic plates collided, thrusting upward a vast plateau. It was this huge block that the Colorado River, seen at left, sculpted for six million years, patiently if relentlessly cleaving a fissure a mile deep and 277 miles long. The record of this passage is indelibly wrought on the exposed rock of the canyon's walls. It is a tale that is constantly respun as shifting sunlight alters the vision over and again.

Otherworldly Bryce Canyon, Lordly Grand Teton

Paiute Indians, whose land this was, had a succinct description for
the fantastic formations that fill Bryce Amphitheater: "red rocks
standing like men in a bowl-shaped canyon." When Utahans boosted
the area for federal recognition in 1919, they called it the Temple
of the Gods. All who have beheld this artwork—rendered by millions
of years of erosion, a panorama still in progress—have found that
words fall short. A no less dramatic landscape is that of Wyoming's
Grand Teton National Park, with rugged peaks jutting nearly 7,000
feet above the valley and the headwaters of the Snake River.

O Shenandoah!

Unique among its brethren, Shenandoah National Park is 194,630 acres of natural splendor that once was home to hundreds of Virginians and host to scores of farming and logging operations. The state acquired the land piece by piece—3,870 privately owned parcels in all—then presented the finished quilt to the federal government as a gift. Shenandoah was established in 1935 after more than 2,000 citizens had been moved from the mountains (some old-timers were allowed to live out their lives within park boundaries, and are in fact buried in Shenandoah graveyards). Skyline Drive affords motorists more than 100 miles of scenic vistas, while the Appalachian Trail, running nearly parallel to it, offers the same sight lines to hikers.

Tim Fitzharris/Minden Pictures

Olympic Gold

"It is not unkind to say, from the standpoint of scenery alone, that if many, and indeed most, of our American national parks were to be set down on the continent of Europe, thousands of Americans would journey all the way across the ocean in order to see their beauties." So said President Franklin D. Roosevelt, who, after visiting Washington's Olympic Peninsula in 1937, ardently supported the movement to make it a national park, which happened the very next year. The only wonder is that it could have taken so long. Olympic is the setting for glacier-capped mountains, a foggy and craggy coastline, and truly remarkable old-growth forests that are home to a dozen or so record-size trees. And, although rainforests are rare in temperate zones, the Hoh, seen here, is an excellent example.

Art Wolfe

National Forests

Yet once more, Theodore Roosevelt figures prominently in the preservation of the American outdoors; one simply has to wonder what this country might look like had it not been for his intense interest in nature. Early in the 20th century, he and his close friend Gifford Pinchot worked hand in glove for long hours to complete transfer of the country's "Forest Reserves" (soon to be the "National Forests") from the aegis of the then fraud-riddled General Land Office to that of Pinchot's Bureau of Forestry. In 1907, two years after the creation of the Forest Service, Chief Forester Pinchot and the President successfully moved to keep 16 million new acres of forest from falling into the grip of the timber syndicates. There are today 155 national forests, which account for 8.2 percent of the U.S. land area. These are public lands that are managed for the multiple uses of recreation,

Jim Brandenburg/Minden Pictures

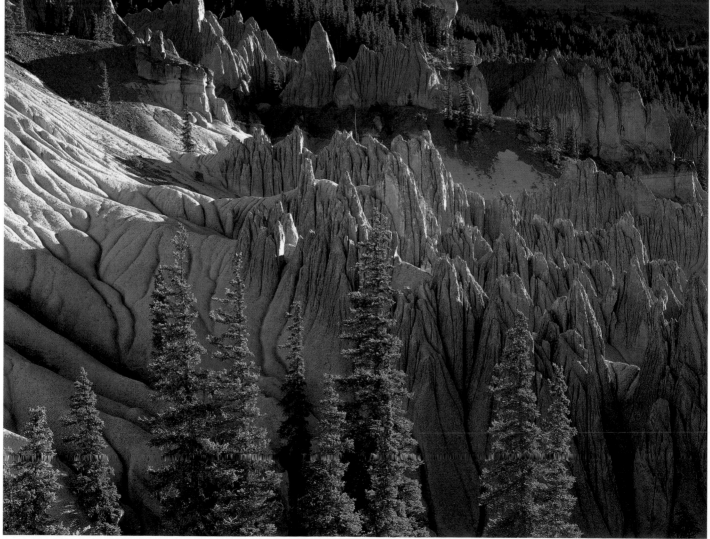

C rr Clifton/Minden Pictures (2)

wildlife, timber, grazing, mining, oil and gas, watershed and wilderness. The Forest Service motto is, Caring for the land and serving people. Above: Vibrant aspens decorate Boulder Mountain in Utah's Dixie National Forest. With nearly two million acres, Dixie includes parts of Bryce Canyon and Zion national parks. At right, autumn holds forth along the Swift River in White Mountain National Forest, located in New Hampshire and Maine; much of the nation's water supply flows from Forest Service lands. At left, the Wheeler Geologic Area in Colorado's Rio Grande National Forest contains volcanic tuff that erodes easily, hence these unlikely formations. Top left: Gray wolves like these bounding through Superior National Forest in Minnesota have been reclassified there, from Endangered to Threatened. As the naturalist Bob Ferris wrote, "Wolves are very resourceful. All they need to survive is for people not to shoot them."

The Crusading Ansel Adams

He was loud and soft, gentle and fierce. He was as deep and complex as the work that he is justly famous for.

Writers, artists and photographers whose focus is the natural world are seldom impartial. They are, by and large, of a conservationist bent, and do not conceal their feelings. Ansel Adams, the iconic photographer of America's most iconic landscapes, was a bear of a man, with a sweet disposition—on the one hand. On the other, he was a firebrand, a zealot, a crusader with his camera every bit as much as Rachel

Carson was with her pen. "Ansel was a mild-mannered guy with a steel psyche," his friend and fellow photographer David Hume Kennerly recalled. "In his opinion you were either for preserving the environment, or against it. There was very little middle ground as far as he was concerned."

Born in San Francisco in 1902, Adams disdained formal education and was allowed by his parents to leave school in 1915; tutors picked up the slack. The following year the Adamses took a

An Artist at Work
"In my mind's eye, I visualize how a particular . . . sight and feeling will appear on a print. If it excites me, there is a good chance it will make a good photograph."
Opposite: Yosemite.

family trip to Yosemite, and Ansel was mesmerized. He returned each summer thereafter, taking pictures in and around the valley. He didn't necessarily see this as a career; in fact, in 1925 he bought a piano, figuring music might be his professional course. He was still undecided when, in 1930, he was deeply influenced by the realistic, "straight" photography of a new friend, Paul Strand. While Adams would continue to play the piano, the camera would from then on be his primary instrument of expression.

He took on commercial and journalistic assignments through the years—shooting everything from raisin bread for an ad to the Mormons of Utah for LIFE—but principally to pay the bills. His

Detail and Vista

Above: Saguaro National Park; right: Yosemite. "In some photographs the essence of light and space dominate; in others, the substance of rock and wood, and the luminous insistence of growing things."

artistic, large-format photography of nature, shot for the Sierra Club or for himself, was the work by which Adams wished to be judged.

"My approach to photography is based on my belief in the aspects of grandeur and minutiae all about us," he once said. As the statement implies, Adams is often misunderstood. The widely circulated posters and calendars featuring massive monoliths and enormous western skies do not represent the whole of Adams. He could thunder like Lear, but he could write a sonnet, too, and any natural realm east, west, north or south was his studio. He shot details; he shot in color. The whole of Adams's portfolio is a revelation.

While Adams subtly lobbied the general public with his images, he bluntly lobbied parks super-

Moments of Rapture

"Landscape photography is the supreme test of the photographer—and often the supreme disappointment." Surely the master was not dismayed by these efforts, above at Glacier, and opposite, a color study of his beloved Yosemite.

intendents, bureaucrats and even world leaders with his words. Kennerly was present at the White House one day when Adams challenged President Gerald R. Ford to do more, declaring, "What we need is women's liberation intensity as far as preservation of our parks is concerned."

"Nobody ever accused Ansel of mincing words!" Kennerly remembered. And nobody ever accused him of lacking impact. In 1976, President Ford, standing in Yellowstone (where he had been a young park ranger), said he would submit to Congress the 10-year, $1.5 billion Bicentennial Land Heritage Act, intended to double the acreage in national parks, recreation areas and wildlife sanctuaries. Ansel Adams died in 1984—his legacy keeping his quest alive.

Polychrome Pass in Denali National Park offers a glimpse of the diversity and drama that is Alaska. From the placid Plains of Murie rises the gigantic Alaska Range, realm of the storied mountain Denali. Moose and wolf and bear coexist here, though not congenially.

Alaska
A Land Apart
Glaciers, Grizzlies and Mystical Mountains

Modes of Transport

Getting about in backcountry Alaska is exhilarating, if not easy. Left: A snowbound safari makes its way through part of what is now Wrangell–St. Elias National Park. Above: In 1940 cartographer Bradford Washburn leads a first ascent up the ridges of Mount Bertha on the Fairweather Peninsula, today part of Glacier Bay. For Washburn and his bride, Barbara (both sporting nifty shades), it is a honeymoon trip. Right: A motorist takes in Denali.

Americans, and this is a true shame.

For decades, the mountain itself and the land surrounding Denali—a term the native Athabaskans used, which means "the high one"—constituted Alaska's only national park. It was established in 1917 as Mount McKinley National Park, settlers having renamed Denali after the 25th U.S. President. North America's highest mountain at 20,320 feet, and the world's tallest from base to summit, it had only recently been conquered; in 1913 three Americans had mounted the first successful expedition. Among them was dog-musher Harry Karstens, who would be the park's first superintendent, charged with managing a spectacular subarctic wilderness and its moose, caribou, Dall sheep, grizzly bears and wolves.

Denali was joined in one fell swoop by seven other enormous parks in 1980 when, after a decade's debate over who was entitled to the Last Frontier—developers? Native Americans? all citizens? small critters and big beasts?—Congress's compromise took shape in the Alaska Lands Act. Under the law's stipulations, Denali increased in size to 6,028,091 acres. Also given park status were 8,500,000 acres in the mountainous north, called Gates of the Arctic; 3,280,198 acres in the south, called Glacier Bay; 4,090,000 acres surrounding volcanic Mount Katmai in the southwest; 573,000 acres in the Kenai Fjords; 1,750,000 acres in the Kobuk Valley; 4,045,000 acres around scenic Lake Clark; and a whopping 13,188,000 acres of mountains and glaciers called Wrangell–St. Elias National Park. On December 2, 1980, wilderness, and Alaska, were exalted.

There are 83.3 million acres of national parkland in the U.S. Nearly half—41.5 million acres—are in Alaska. As this implies, everything there is vaster and arguably more awe-inspiring than almost anything in the Lower 48. Everything is also much colder, wilder and more remote, with the majority of parks accessible only by boat or plane. The consequence is that relatively few of the nation's citizens ever experience this extraordinary world. Consider: In 2002, Alaska's busiest park, Denali, hosted 280,911 visitors—or not quite 3 percent of the total at Great Smoky Mountains National Park. A most marvelous part of America is never seen by most

The Denizens of Denali

Summer invites human guests, to gawk and take pictures, but during the seasons of darkness and cold these residents are on their own, to survive or not, to prey and be preyed upon. King of Predators is Griz, who can reach 35 mph and tear apart a half-ton moose in no time; one wants to avoid a wounded *Ursus arctos horribilis,* or one with her cubs. The Denali food chain descends through 37 species of mammal, down to pikas, hoary marmots, ground squirrels and snowshoe hares. Meadows below Denali's twin peaks nurture a large moose population, while the high country harbors Dall sheep, kin to the bighorn.

Wrangell–St. Elias: The Behemoth

In preparing a volume such as this, one must at times resort to superlatives. With Wrangell–St. Elias, we are at the nonpareil of national parks, if only in the sense that the scale of it easily surpasses any other. Nearly half a dozen Yellowstone National Parks could fit inside Wrangell–St. Elias, which is known as "the mountain kingdom of North America." The park holds nine of the 16 tallest summits in the U.S., including 18,008-foot Mount St. Elias, the second highest in the nation. Mount Wrangell is one of the largest active volcanoes in North America, while Nabesna is the world's longest nonpolar valley glacier and Bagley the largest nonpolar ice field. Malaspina Glacier is bigger than the state of Rhode Island. And, of course, the wildlife is bountiful in the extreme.

Marc Muench

Carr Clifton/Minden Pictures

Kobuk Valley and Glacier Bay: Marked Contrast

The 49th state is host to a splendid array of diverse natural features, as evidenced in these photographs. A large part of the southern Kobuk Valley (below) is covered with sand that was formed by the grinding of ancient glaciers, then transported to the park by wind and water. The many dunes butt up against vegetation, which serves as a natural stabilizer. Right: Glacier Bay boasts steep, snowcapped mountain ranges as well as deep fjords. It also affords a superb opportunity for studying the generation of flora and fauna in the wake of retreating glaciers. Here, a sunset view of beached glacial ice at Muir Inlet, in Glacier Bay's East Arm.

Michael Melford

Michael Melford (2)

Gates of the Arctic: Pristine Paradise

Situated in north-central Alaska's Brooks Range, Gates of the Arctic comprises a national park, national preserve, six Wild Rivers and two national natural landmarks. This is virginal territory, a radiant wilderness of glaciated valleys and heroic peaks. Bob Marshall, the restless, charismatic founder of the Wilderness Society, gave the area its name, and planted the seeds for its survival. At left, the limpid waters of the Alatna are the paradigm of a meandering river. Above, a sublime setting for aurora borealis. Below, caribou on the fly. This park has the requisite seclusion that permits the presence of the most secretive of animals, including the fierce, wily wolverine.

Fred Hirschmann

Katmai National Park—Rugged, Untamed

It is as well that the governor of the Alaska territory, Thomas C. Riggs, went unheeded when he stated in 1919: "Katmai National Monument serves no use and should be abolished." Had anyone listened to Riggs, development would have imperiled these grizzlies and sockeye salmon, this tableau in the River Lethe. Nor would we have these words from Gilbert E. Blinn, Katmai's first superintendent: "It is a land of uncrowded spaciousness, a place where people can experience wilderness on its own terms without the distraction of hordes of other visitors. It is a place where time and change are measured by the sun, the tides and the seasons rather than clocks and calendars."

Michael Melford

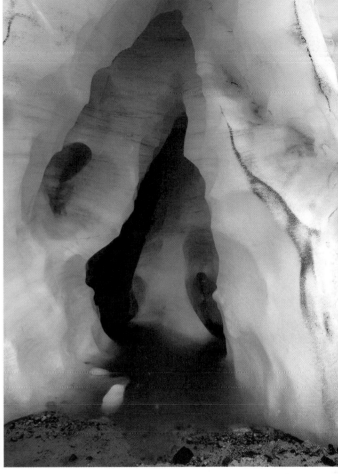

Fred Hirschmann

Kenai Fjords: A World Defined by Water

The photograph at left nicely demonstrates that a glacier is in essence a river, if a slow-moving one. Active bodies of ice, these massive, grinding flows leave behind ponds and lakes, canyons and valleys. Much of the topography of the upper half of North America has been shaped by glaciers, which are the earth's most powerful practitioners of erosion. The fjords of Kenai are long valleys that were etched by glaciers and now are filled with seawater. The dark stripes in the glacier at left are known as medial moraines, which are created by the confluence of two or more valley or outlet glaciers. Above, an ice cave that has been sculpted in Aialik Bay. Kenai Fjords' wildlife includes hardy creatures that have survived in a narrow zone between marine waters and the frozen perimeter of a huge ice field.

Issues Today

It is not all sunny skies, clean water, well-fed critters and shiny, happy people in the parks. In fact, air pollution is a problem from California to Tennessee. Water degradation due to encroaching sprawl threatens habitats not just in famous wetlands like Everglades but in wildlife preserves coast to coast. As for flora and fauna, the introduction of "exotic" or nonindigenous plants and animals, from creeping kudzu plants to zebra mussels, poses serious problems to native species in half of all National Park Service holdings. And as regards people: In some places, there are simply too many of them. Among the issues now generating headlines is noise pollution caused by small-plane and helicopter flyovers of the Grand Canyon (above, left); environmentalists have gone to court to try to further limit the number of tourist flights now allowed by the Federal Aviation Administration. In Yellowstone, a snowmobile phaseout plan proposed by the Clinton administration was halted in 2002 by President Bush's Interior and Justice departments. (Critics say the machines

pollute, and disturb the park's bison, as they certainly seem to be doing in the photo at left.) There has been a controversial proposal to allow snowmobiles in Alaska's Denali as well, and it is clear that users of off-road vehicles, like the wheelie-popper at Everglades, opposite, will continue to press for more park access in years ahead. Many of the famous parks are, quite plainly, overcrowded and overtaxed in summer, which leads to traffic snarls, degradation of trails and off-trail environments and a general erosion of the "wilderness experience." (Exhibit A: campers at Redwood National Park, above.) Last but not least, there's the issue of safety. The parks, after all, are wide-open spaces. The case of Cary Stayner, who drew a death sentence for the 1999 murders of three Yosemite tourists and a park guide, focused attention on an issue that had only been whispered about: a disturbing, modern-day uptick in crime in the parks. These places may be paradise, but they are of the real world.

Richard Darby/AP

The Intrepid Galen Rowell

A mountaineer who was a photographer—and vice versa—viewed the parks from an entirely new vantage.

First there were landscape photographers, then came nature photographers. In recent years a new breed has appeared on the outdoor scene: the adventure photographer. Galen Rowell, a hybrid of the tough-as-nails climber and the poetic lensman, was a master of all three forms.

Born in 1940, he grew up in the hills of Berkeley, Calif., possessed of boundless energy. For a time, he expended that zeal at the wheel of hot rods. Among the grumbling neighbors whenever Galen went bombing down the street was the famous outdoorsman and environmental activist David Brower. Later, when Rowell had calmed down a tad, he found inspiration in Brower's life and came to consider the older man a "shadow

Portrait of the Artist as an Adventurous Man
Yosemite was as sacred to Rowell as it had been to fellow Bay Area native Ansel Adams (above, Rowell hanging out near Yosemite Falls in 1992). In his world travels, Galen was usually accompanied by the equally adventurous Barbara (left). Opposite: alpenglow on a corniced ridge of Alaska's Denali.

Robert W. Tope

Ron Kauk

In the Picture

In certain frames, it is evident that Rowell is part of the action. Here, a climbing partner makes his way down to the Peter's Glacier, which resides high on a Denali flank.

mentor" in both rock climbing and photography.

Rowell ran an auto-parts and service shop for a decade but was continually trying to stretch weekends into four days in the mountains. Shortly after his 30th birthday, he looked around and realized that what he loved doing—adventure photography—wasn't being done by many other people, yet there seemed to be a growing market for it. So he headed for the hills, and within a year

saw his bank account dwindle to $50. Then came an assignment for *National Geographic,* and Rowell was on his way.

He put his personal, very creative spin on the standard scenics—El Capitan from the valley, sunset on the Tetons—but it was the photographs taken at elevation that amazed. They were, without doubt, wonderfully composed. And then, invariably, after a few moments . . . "Wait," the question

dawned on the viewer. "Where was the photographer? How did the photographer get there?"

He got there the way any world-class climber would: ropes, courage, daring, skill and muscle—with danger as a constant companion. Over three decades, Rowell made more than 20 expeditions in the Himalayas, as well as trips to both poles; he scaled mountains in Patagonia and trekked through Africa. In his lifetime he registered more

than 100 first ascents worldwide. But such a résumé—an adventurer's résumé—tends to distract attention from the art, which was always superb.

On August 11, 2002, Galen Rowell and his wife, Barbara, who was also a photographer, were killed when the twin-engine plane in which they were traveling crashed in California. Their friends were shocked. The Rowells had survived a river-

New Perspectives

In the pre-Rowell era, most scenics of Mount Huntington in Denali National Park (top) and Mount Whitney in California's Sequoia were taken from the valley floor below.

Straightforward, but Hardly Ordinary

While very little outdoor work is as distinctive as Rowell's adventure portfolio, his landscapes also display an individual approach to light and color—as here in Yosemite (below), Yellowstone (bottom) and California's Kings Canyon. In 2001, at the age of 61, the globe-jaunting Rowell wrote: "I've known all along that more of what I am seeking in the wilds is right here in my home state of California than anywhere else on earth."

running accident in the Andes in which Barbara had fractured her skull, and Galen had emerged from more scrapes than could be counted. In a moving reminiscence, Ken Brower, David's son, wrote, "That these two should perish in an event as mundane as a plane crash does not quite make sense. They should have somehow finessed themselves out of that falling plane, like the Houdinis they were." In summation, Brower offered a hopeful vision of his late father, and his late friend. "If my theory about heaven is correct, climbers are not allowed to bring a lot of technical hardware along with them. The ascents are pure, the way Rowell and Brower liked it, and those two are now busy bouldering there."

The relentless power of the Pacific surf infuses this still (for the moment) life photograph taken on Hidden Beach in northern California's Redwood National Park. In the foreground is a long-fallen redwood, reclining now on a rocky bed.

1946-2003
The Next Wave

A Revolutionary Idea Is Refined.

Previous pages: Carr Clifton/Minden Pictures

t is ironic that during a dire period in America's history—the Great Depression—the parks prospered, their infrastructure polished to a fine sheen. And during the rah-rah post–World War II years, they slumped. That all energy and expenditure had been redirected to the military effort was understandable. But even with the war over, it proved exceedingly hard to turn Washington's attention back to such topics as conservation and preservation. The parks, all but abandoned from 1942 through '45, remained neglected and underfunded as America busied itself with the cold and Korean wars.

In the 1950s, Park Service director Conrad L. Wirth began pushing a 10-year plan to shore up the system. His words fell on deaf congressional ears until a series of articles awakened the public to the rot that threatened the nation's crown jewels. "Let's Close Our National Parks" was the sarcastic title of a piece by Bernard De Voto in the October 1953 *Harper's.* In April 1954, *Travel* ran Jerome Wood's "National Parks Tomorrow's Slums?" And in January 1955, Charles Stevenson's

"The Shocking Truth About Our National Parks" appeared in far-reaching *Reader's Digest.* A chorus of protest swelled; Congress got religion.

Wirth's plan eventually cost more than a billion dollars, and the parks grew strong on the money, then were fed—psychically, physically, financially—by the 1960s environmental revolution. Rachel Carson's warnings were in the air, and the ideas of such as naturalist Aldo Leopold had sway at the Park Service. On the other hand, the lofty goals of "preservation" and "education" again clashed with "recreation," as scads of baby boomers on vacation demanded fun, fun, fun.

The Park Service tried to strike a balance—or to tip it—as its system grew, with ever more diverse ecosystems added in the modern era. The few set-asides of the 1940s and '50s—Big Bend on Texas's Rio Grande in 1944, Florida's Everglades in '47, the Virgin Islands in '56—were joined, in the 1960s, '70s and particularly in 1980—by a host of new-wave parks: Haleakala in Hawaii ('61); Arizona's Petrified Forest ('62); Utah's Canyonlands ('64); Washington's North

Different Habitats

In the beginning, it was clear that a locale had to have something really big or otherwise mind-boggling to qualify as a national park—a sensational waterfall, say, or a staggering mountain; a geyser would come in handy. But after World War II, new ecological thinking led to the protection of exotics like the Everglades, as well as coral seas and bone-dry deserts.

Old Trees, New Life

Some venerable landmarks came late to their park status. In 1962, 93,533 acres of fossilized wood and Indian ruins in Arizona were set aside as the Petrified Forest (right). Six years later, 108,400 acres of ancient trees in California became Redwood National Park. Below: In 1925 parks chief Stephen Mather (left) poses at a redwood with timber baron John Emmert and Secretary of the Interior Hubert Work.

Cascades and California's Redwood ('68); Utah's Arches and Capitol Reef (both '71); Guadalupe Mountains in Texas ('72); Voyageurs in Minnesota ('75); the Dakotas' Badlands and Theodore Roosevelt (both '78). In 1980, as we've seen, the Alaska Lands Act added hugely to the Park Service's treasure. That same year, Florida's Biscayne was upgraded from national monument to park, and California's Channel Islands joined the system as well. In 1986, Nevada's Great Basin was established, as was a national park in American Samoa in 1988. In 1992, Dry Tortugas off Key West gained protection, as did, in '94, a lot of dry desert in three parks: California's Joshua Tree and Death Valley, and Arizona's Saguaro. The two youngest national parks are the Black Canyon of the Gunnison in Colorado, added in 1999, and Cuyahoga Valley, established in 2000. The former is in the classic, dramatic park mold, while the latter comprises 33,000 relatively mild acres between Cleveland and Akron where the visitor can picnic, bike, fish or . . . golf. The reinvention of America's best idea continues. Fore!

The Ballad of Big Bend

When the West was wild, the Tex-Mex borderland near the big southward bend in the Rio Grande River was the wildest. Comanches launched raids from the dusty Chihuahuan Desert on usurping white ranchers and Mexican villages. But rustlers were thick as rattlers, and as recently as 1917, Black Jack Pershing was chasing Pancho Villa around the Bend. During Prohibition the border was a faucet for tequila. Texas acquired much of this land between 1933 and '44, then gave it to the feds, who established a park. Big Bend's serenity today—yuccas (right), the Chisos Mountains, 450 bird species (more than any other national park), the river itself—is a sublime counterpoint to the raucous past.

Carr Clifton/Minden Pictures

The Essential Ecology of Everglades

On the southern tip of the Florida peninsula, Everglades National Park yields one of the planet's foremost sites for wildlife. The "River of Grass" is an avian haven, featuring such waders as the roseate spoonbill, reddish egret and tricolored heron (seen stalking at right). Among 14 endangered species clinging to life here are the Florida panther and the American crocodile. North America's only subtropical preserve, the park supports nine different plant habitats, including mangrove forest, cypress swamp and saw-grass prairie. The Everglades is involved in what is likely a never-ending battle, as the needs of South Florida's human population continue to grow.

The Ancient Petrified Forest

A decidedly unusual and fascinating national park is resident in northeastern Arizona. Petrified Forest is an artifact land from another time, home to remnants of a world that existed 225 million years ago. In the southern region of the park, one finds petrified wood like the segment at right that suggests nothing so much as a living-color pillar from a classical temple, toppled now but its majesty intact, adorned with resplendent quartz that long ago replaced the wood tissue. In the northern section of Petrified Forest is the Painted Desert, with its rugose badlands (below) marked throughout with striations of color. These mounds are mainly sedimentary rock with a high content of bentonite clay, which swells when wet, then settles as it dries. The Anasazi petroglyph at left incorporates features of both a mountain lion and a bighorn sheep.

The Captivating Canyonlands

Ancestors of this mountain lion have been prowling the area of Utah now called Canyonlands since long before human hunter-gatherers first happened upon the site 10,000 years ago. It was many moons later, in 1869, that John Wesley Powell began a three-month exploration of the Green and Colorado rivers, which converge here. The landscape had a singular effect on Powell, as he recorded in his diary : " . . . rock—cliffs of rock; plateaus of rock; terraces of rock; crags of rock—ten thousand strangely carved forms." It is a terrain of sedimentary sandstone molded through time into mesas, buttes and canyons bounded by sheer walls. While there are four distinct areas, there is throughout a shared element of primitive desert that is characterized by cactus, cottonwood and coyote. The light is always at work at Canyonlands, as seen here with the first moments of dawn attending to Mesa Arch, one of the wonders in the district known as Island in the Sky.

Carr Clifton/Minden Pictures

Chuck Davis

Colossal Forests: Redwood and Channel Islands

These two parks are both in California, and both are home to titans, but as one can see, they are very different places. Above, sunlight filters through the fronds of a giant kelp forest off Santa Barbara Island, one of five isles that make up Channel Islands National Park. Kelp is seaweed that employs its rootlike holdfasts to cling to rocky subaquatic surfaces; its tangled tendrils, which can reach 100 feet, create a cool, dark microenvironment ideal for a food chain that stretches from plankton to crabs to octopuses to blue whales—along with oodles of fish, which is what this California sea lion has in mind. At left, an elegant rhododendron sparkles in an array of Redwood National Park's old-growth trees, which can live for 2,000 years and surpass 300 feet.

The Hawaiian Eden: Haleakala

Sited on Maui, Haleakala bursts with tropical pulchritude. Mark Twain, after seeing a sunrise there, said, "I felt like the Last Man, neglected of the judgment, and left pinnacled in mid-heaven, a forgotten relic of a vanished world." Twain called Vesuvius a "modest pit," and Kilauea "somewhat deeper . . . But what are either of them compared to the vacant stomach of Haleakala? . . . It must have afforded a spectacle worth contemplating in the old days when its furnaces gave full rein to their anger." Many locals regard this Hawaiian short-eared owl as a guardian spirit. One hopes that it will provide succor in the crusade against introduced species.

Theodore Roosevelt and Kindred Spirits

Teddy Roosevelt was one of America's preeminent defenders of wilderness, thus it is entirely fitting that his Elkhorn Ranch in North Dakota be set aside as a national park. Another prime spirit of the American outdoors is also here: the bison, sine qua non for the Plains Indian and one of the animals most linked to the young nation. Twelve feet long and capable of weighing more than a ton, the bison is the largest mammal in North America, yet surprisingly fast and agile. The long-lived, social creatures do well wherever there is forage, water and space—and no one to hunt them to near extinction. Wolf, coyote and bear pursue them, but without the wantonness displayed by European immigrants in the 19th century. Almost all wild bison now live in protected areas.

Desert Oases: Joshua Tree and Death Valley

Death Valley (right) is famed around the world for its spectacular scenery and complex geology. It is the hottest, driest and lowest spot in the United States. But with less extravagant desert areas, like Joshua Tree National Park, first-time visitors sometimes depart with a ho-hum feeling; the sights there don't make you gasp in awe. It is, however, precisely this kind of place where each return venture permits a deeper understanding and appreciation for the setting and its life-forms. And because this place grows on you, there can develop a personal response, an emotion, perhaps even an intimacy; you can fall in love with a place like this. At left, a garden of teddy bear cholla.

Jeff Gnass

David Muench

The Badlands, and the Good

The interior of North America was once dense with forest,
but 64 million years ago the Rocky Mountains and Black
Hills slowly began to rise, and moisture drifting east from
the Pacific ran into a rock wall. Woodlands failed, and
tough grasses took their place. Just about everything in
South Dakota's Badlands National Park has developed
over millions of years: the Oligocene Epoch fossil record
that whispers of the weird ancient forebears of the horse,
pig, sheep and even rhinoceros; the barren terrain (called
mako sica, or "land bad," by the Sioux) that spreads
out from the Black Hills; and the 56 different grasses
that survive east of the mountains, constituting one of
the largest protected mixed-grass prairies in the U.S.

Tim Fitzharris/Minden Pictures

Carr Clifton/Minden Pictures

Just One More

Raise Your Voices!

Home, home on the range
Where the deer and the antelope
(And the bison and the bighorn
And the griz and the ground squirrel
And almost 700 other mammals—
Including this black-tailed prairie dog
At Wind Cave National Park
In South Dakota—
Not to mention all the fish
And birds of the air)
Plaaaaay!
Where seldom is heard
A discouraging word
And the skies are not cloudy all day . . .

Jim Brandenburg/Minden Pictures